CW00820807

Let go of What Hurts You and Master your Emotions

Don't let negative thinking define your future. Focus on how to manage your emotional thoughts

By

Emily J. Greyson

© **Copyright 2022 by Emily J. Greyson - All rights reserved**.

This document is geared towards providing exact and reliable information regarding the topic and issue covered.

- From a Declaration of Principles which was accepted and approved equally by a Committee of the American Bar Association and a Committee of Publishers and Associations.

In no way is it legal to reproduce, duplicate, or transmit any part of this document in either electronic means or printed format. All rights reserved.

The information provided herein is stated to be truthful and consistent. Any liability, in terms of inattention or otherwise, by any usage or abuse of any policies, processes, or directions contained within is the solitary and utter responsibility of the recipient reader. Under no circumstances will any legal obligation or blame be held against the publisher for any reparation, damages, or monetary loss due to the information herein, either directly or indirectly.

Respective authors own all copyrights not held by the publisher.

The information herein is solely offered for informational purposes and is universal. The presentation of the data is without a contract or any guaranteed assurance.

The trademarks that are used are without any consent, and the publication of the trademark is without permission or backing by the trademark owner. All trademarks and brands within this book are for clarifying purposes only and are owned by themselves, not affiliated with this document.

Inside you will find instructions for getting a small notebook for free with some "Famous Phrases," on which you can do the exercises or jot down your emotions, reflections or gratitude.

Affectionately

Emily J. Greyson

Contents

9

Introduction

Our peace of mind is our direct responsibility. There is no more important thing or person than our psychological well-being. We cannot allow the actions of others to upset our emotions. Our lives depend on our own actions, not those of others. Understanding this assumption of responsibility, on me, had a liberating effect. My serenity, my anger, my frustrations, depend on me!

Too often, our thoughts persuade us that others have a certain opinion of us, or judge us for our actions or demand something of us. We persuade ourselves that others think what our minds suggest. But in most situations, it is we ourselves who judge ourselves first and experience the discomfort that sometimes leads us to reactions that are not consistent with reality.

Reason why the first step is to learn to love and respect ourselves without judgment toward ourselves and others. We must learn to love ourselves at such a deep level that we do not look for the certainties around us, because the certainties are within us.

Choosing to be responsible for our own happiness also means taking all those events that happened to us in the past and changing their meaning, looking at them from another perspective to credit them for the strengths we have today so that we can free ourselves, instead, from the burden of negative emotions attached to them.

I know that playing the victim, feeling sorry for ourselves, thinking and rethinking in trying to blame others for our unhappiness, is much easier. But one can choose to remain succubus to situations and wallow in sorrow, or one can choose to give a completely different meaning to what one has experienced so far and realize that one is happy anyway because of what are events in our past.

One can learn to manage one's emotions, to reconcile with oneself, to love and respect oneself. "Emotions are for living life not suffering it!"

We can learn not to judge ourselves and others, to control and manage our anger, and above all to be our own priority.

I am not saying that this is an easy and immediate change, but you can choose to do it and, more importantly, you can start doing it.

These pages that follow, are not meant to presume to transform your life, but to give you a push toward change, even including by way of small suggestions and exercises, that is!

Chapter 1: Stop Overthinking To Alter Your Life By Changing Your Ideas

"Overthinking ruins you. It ruins the situation. And it twists things around. It makes you worry. Plus, it makes everything worse than it is."- Karen Salmansohn.

Humans are quite effective at finding solutions to issues with limited variables. It includes going to the store, doing laundry, or making a meal. Other examples include driving to the store. We are also quite skilled at finding solutions to issues that include many variables. Examples include sophisticated works of art, music, architectural designs, and computer programs.

On the other hand, we are not particularly good at finding solutions to challenges involving anything in the middle. For instance, most of us would have difficulty solving a problem with more than three variables without a pencil. A good deal of unease from having a hyperactive mind originates. Our brains put in additional effort to find a solution to an issue with many distinct variables, one that is complicated enough to be difficult and irritating but not so complicated that it prevents our brains from reaching their full creative potential.

Many in the business world refer to this propensity to overthink things as "analysis paralysis," which can be detrimental to one's success. It manifests as mental strain, stress, and lethargy in our daily lives. Put, giving too much thought to everything is uncomfortable and prevents you from going ahead and achieving progress when taken to an excessive degree; overthinking leads you to shut down entirely and totally and results in serious uneasiness.

It is of supreme importance to realize that if you demonstrate a propensity to overthink matters, you are just being human. It is something that you should maintain in mind. There is no problem with it in any way. Our brains are programmed to look for answers whenever we encounter a challenge. We also need to be aware that we can utilize our intelligence and mental function to recognize when we are "spinning our mental wheels" in vain and break free of this way of thinking to move forward.

There are concrete and straightforward approaches to overcoming the tendency to overthink every situation. Read over the following list, and the next time you feel yourself becoming bogged down in your thoughts, choose one of the strategies to use to break free from the shackles of excessive thinking. You will undoubtedly find respite from your tension, and in the process, you could just produce an original answer to the challenge you are facing.

1.1: Release Your Grip On The Outcomes

The Bhagavad Gita, a spiritual classic that has had a significant influence on my life, asserts that we might achieve pleasure and do our duty ("dharma") in life by concentrating only on the needed work that we must perform rather than on the results of the labor that we have performed. Because of the unpredictability of the result, putting too much emphasis on outcomes may be stressful. In contrast, hand, shifting our attention to our task relocates us into the domain of things that are within our command. The end effect is a reduction in mental strain and an improvement in one's capacity to work through difficult difficulties.

1.2: Cultivate Pleasant Feelings

RIP Spike! It might be challenging to overcome bad feelings caused by excessive thinking and the feelings that emerge from it. Quite some time ago, when I had difficulty adjusting to life without Spike, my much-loved dog and closest friend, I saw this myself. After my Love had gone away, I suffered for a few days. My heart was shattered on the inside, and my head was spinning as I considered everything, I might have done differently to preserve his health for a longer period.

During our conversation, my mother shared some information that caused a sea shift in how I felt. She brought to my notice that even though I am going through this difficult time, I must not overlook that there is a person else in my life who needs my attention and care. I also have another dog named Duke, who, even though he undoubtedly missed his older brother, could not communicate his feelings in the same way that people can. I made it my primary concern to ensure Duke received plenty of affection. When I started to feel sorry about Spike and saw that my thoughts were racing and that I was dwelling too much on his death, I turned my attention to Duke. I focused my attention on providing him with the utmost level of care.

15

Because of this change in perspective, the weight of my sadness has been lifted, and my mind has stopped dwelling on the past and making me feel guilty for not having taken better care of his health before his life. I was able to settle down and regain my clarity of thought.

1.3: Carry Out Routine Responsibilities With Full Attention

When I am during difficult work and discover that I am overanalyzing, I often switch to more straightforward and straightforward jobs that need less mental horsepower. For instance, I will walk my dog, mow the grass, take care of some bills, and do the laundry today. The accomplishment of several uncomplicated errands provides me with a sense of fulfillment. I get the sensation that I have achieved something. In addition, it trains my brain to solve difficulties and follow through on tasks. When I go back to the difficult work, such as putting together a presentation, getting ready for a counseling client meeting, or writing on this book, I can maintain my concentration without experiencing mental strain. My thoughts are organized, and I am prepared to do the assignment, regardless of how difficult it may be.

1.4: Meditate

Meditation is somewhat that you should do for a variety of different reasons. The following is a short list of the advantages that have been substantiated by scientific research

- Reduced levels of anxiety
- Reduced levels of depression
- Greater ability to withstand discomfort
- Enhanced capabilities in terms of both memory and learning
- Heightened sense of self-awareness
- Improved ability to determine one's objectives
- Increased sensitivity and compassion
- Higher levels of "alpha" waves lead to decreased stress, melancholy, and rage levels.
- Reduced levels of blood pressure
- Enhanced capabilities in the processing of oxygen and carbon dioxide
- A better immune response function
- Safeguarding both cells and DNA
- Possible health advantages for preventing cancer, diabetes, and cardiovascular disease

Even if you give yourself 10 minutes to meditate, you will notice that your level of overthinking has decreased significantly. The practice of meditation is analogous to looking deep inside yourself and gaining a better understanding of how your life is unfolding. Even a little period of meditation allows one to see the mind's tendency toward excessive thinking. When you have this awareness, all negativity linked with it will go away. Do not worry if you do not know how to meditate; the directions are easy to follow and are located right here.

1.5: Try Not To Consciously Overthink Things

Tony Robbins is the one who taught me how to use this strategy. It is used to break apart old habits of thought and replace them with new patterns of thought that are more powerful. Implementing the concept involves simplifying matters so that you may focus on seeing the comedy in overthinking everything. Because of this, we can only use our highest possible level of innate brilliance when we are in a condition of mental and emotional serenity (I should clarify that I am not referring to our physical health).

Let's imagine you're attempting to prepare a presentation, but you're getting bogged down in how to organize your slides and which tales to tell for the greatest possible effect. Spend a few minutes deliberately overthinking the situation in a conscious and preventative manner. How many ways/tips are there to organize your slides? Which of the many diverse tales that you might tell are your favorites? What are the many activities you might be doing now that would prevent you from concentrating on putting up your presentation? What are the many concerns that individuals who are a part of your audience may have regarding you?

Could you take it to an extreme with this? Look for the funny side of it. Imagine that you have 10 arms and that they are all flailing around and making millions of slides so that you can cover everything. Imagine that you are typing so quickly that the keyboard is starting to smoke and is on the verge of catching fire. Imagine the event playing out in the most ludicrous way possible.

Now that you've calmed down take a good look at the presentation you've prepared. Recognize that excessive thought is not useful in getting your task done. It does nothing except get in your way. Imagine that you are putting together your presentation logically and thoughtfully. Imagine that you are just going about your business without being concerned with the product, doing things one at a time. Return your attention to the subject and begin working with a refreshed awareness of concentration and an at-ease mind.

1.6: Get Some Exercise

Getting enough sleep & engaging in physical activity may be compared to hitting the reset button on your brain. It is impossible to go for a run and then return to your job without having a different set of minds than when you left. When I have a lot of energy that I haven't burnt off, I tend to ponder too much, and this inclination is at its worst for me. If you go outdoors and exercise, you will notice that the mental stress and excessive thinking you experienced before will be gone when you go back inside.

1.7: Take Deep And Even Breaths (Pranayama)

The rhythm and tenor of the breathing are a direct expression of the state of mind you are now in. Don't trust me? Give yourself five full breaths, inhaling and exhaling slowly through your nose. You will certainly recognize a change in how you consider and feel about the situation.

Pranayama is a technique that has been around for an exceptionally long time and is required of individuals who want to explore higher realms of consciousness. Yogis have recognized this secret for a long time, which is why they do it. It is equally significant to engage in physical activity and practice mental meditation.

The practice known as Nadi Shodhana is one of the most effective techniques. After a short period spent doing it, your mind will become very concentrated, much like the Death Star — but positively.

1.8: Make A Habit Of Concentrating Your Eyes On A Single Place

In the same way that the breath can tell a lot about the condition of your mind, your eyes can also tell a great deal about the state of your soul, as some people think. Eye contact is avoided by many yogis who are deeply involved in their spiritual training for this reason; it is a portal to your inner self. Fixing your gaze (without staring, of course!) has been shown to have a calming and concentrating effect on the mind. Whether you presume this or not, it is a widely held belief that, in the same way, the eyes and their temperamental movement indicate that the mind is overactive, so too can fixing your gaze.

Exercising the habit of fixing your gaze on a single location for a period will help you think less and feel more relaxed. I would rather perform this workout outside in the fresh air. I will focus on anything as simple as a tree, a blade of grass, a cloud, and even an animal. Make sure that your eyes are not getting tired from focusing too hard. Keep your usual blinking pattern and maintain a calm and relaxed look. Your mind will become more at ease (and focused!) in direct proportion to the degree to which your eyes can relax.

1.9: Put Your Ideas And Thoughts Down On Paper

Have you ever heard of the newspaper called "Morning Pages"? The practice consists of writing three pages first thing in the morning without editing or censoring anything that comes out. Morning Pages is a practice popularized by Julia Cameron, who refers to it as "the core of creative recovery". My experience has shown that putting one's ideas into paper, regardless of the time of day, may assist unload an overthinking mind, aid in concentration, and alleviate tension. Getting into the routine of writing first thing in the morning has several benefits, one of which is that it may prevent the anxious, overactive mind from ever showing its ugly face later in the day!

1.10: Take a Snooze

A good nap is always welcome! Just like exercise, a 20-minute snooze works wonders. After getting in a good run and refueling with a nutritious smoothie, one of my favorite times to sleep is in the afternoon, around 3 o'clock. I don't think there's much more I need to say about naps; you should give it a go!

1.11: Change your Surroundings

It is stated that Albert Einstein, when he was laboring to develop his theory of relativity, had his greatest breakthrough while taking a break from concentrating on his issue to rest and daydream while sitting by a fire. Altering one's surroundings may do wonders to foster the development of novel ways of thinking. When trying to look at the stars in the night sky, you won't be able to see them if you look at them straight on, but you will be able to see them if you move your eyes to the periphery of your field of vision.

If you notice that you are thinking too much, switching up your surroundings may help. It would be finest if you went to a park, a coffee shop, or the library. Put down the keyboard and pick up some pencils and paper instead. Surround yourself with individuals different from you and engage in conversations on novel topics. Put an end to your active efforts to solve the issue and daydream instead.

Chapter 2: Break Free From Shackles Of The Past

"Expectations are the shackles that will not permit something to be what it is."— Craig D. Lounsbrough

Most people, at some point in their lives, have pondered the question of how to move on from a painful previous experience. It is only natural/normal for you to feel that the source of the emotional agony you are experiencing now lies in the past. However, even if it happened in the past, the first step in overcoming the pain is concentrating on the present. The inquiry of how to move on from the past will likely be interpreted differently by everyone.

It could also depend on the circumstances of the case. You could believe that letting go means being capable of remembering painful situations or individuals without feeling the associated emotional pain. It's possible that you feel like it's about forgetting everything. Alternatively, it could suggest that you wish to move on even though you haven't forgotten or forgiven the person yet. It is possible to let go of whatever is weighing heavily on your heart and head, whatever that may mean to you. You can heal, and the following advice may be of assistance to you.

1. Questioning

You may become accustomed to your emotional anguish when you've been injured for a long enough. Perhaps you have a sense of comfort and recognition. You may have accepted it as a fundamental aspect of your identity. Keeping your anger at

26

that individual may make you feel more secure since it allows you to maintain your distance from them. The discomfort of maturing can be quite genuine. It's possible that walking away from something you've been thinking and feeling for an exceptionally long time can make you feel uneasy. On the other hand, it's possible that letting go will lead to healing, joy, and mental tranquility. It's possible that this won't be the case for everybody, but if you find yourself asking, "Why can't I let go?" the following questions may be able to assist you in starting to let go of the past: Does maintaining your attention on the painful aspects of the situation result in any further benefits?

Does dwelling on the past prevent you from pursuing new romantic partnerships or professional opportunities? Do you postpone resolving emotional distress because you know it will require you to confront it? What would change in your life if you decided to let the past stay in the past? What do you guess the effects would be if you played a different part in the scenario?

2. Consider Letting It Out

Sometimes, to heal, you must first allow yourself to feel it. It may be more detrimental to you long-term and make it difficult to let go if you bottle up your sentiments and thoughts. It is especially true if you keep considering the past and the things that have wronged you. Your mood, relationship, and even your capacity to be creative and efficient might be negatively impacted if you repeatedly think about the same bad emotions. It would improve if you tried to find healthy ways to convey your feelings. Getting rid of the emotional energy could make it easier for you to cease ruminating. Think about participating in activities that will allow you to vent your emotions in a protected environment. Keeping a journal that includes prompts is one example. Expressing your anguish through art or enjoy if writing or talking is complicated for you. Find a friend, relative, or psychiatrist to share your feelings and emotions with. Put in writing a letter to the person who upset you. Expressing your pain through art or play may be less difficult than trying to write or speak.

3. Consider Taking Accountability

Taking accountability for your actions does not callous you have to accept blame for events that occurred to you in the past. The primary step in this process is to realize how much energy you devote to thinking or hearing emotions that are no longer part of your present. It also involves making the conscious decision to direct your attention elsewhere. When you let go of your hurt, resentment, or painful memories, you repeatedly force yourself to relive an unpleasant experience. It may cause you to remain mired there in the past. That is something that has passed and cannot be altered. Accepting responsibility means claiming his power and deciding that you will not allow others to control where you feel or how you conduct your life. It's possible that you didn't have a choice in the matters that caused you pain in the past, so you do now. You have a choice today about where you will place your thoughts and feelings. The perception that this is a challenging undertaking is normal and appropriate. Either the anguish is so excruciating that you can't help but concentrate on it, or you have no alternative but to deal with the repercussions of your actions. However, there is still hope for healing. You might want to talk to a professional therapist about improving your ability to deal with difficult situations and how this can make it easier for you to let go of the past.

4. Space

When you fixate on things that have happened in the past, you might not have much room in your heart and head for new experiences, especially ones that might offer you joy. Your inability to release yourself from the past may increase the likelihood that you will overlook the positive aspects of your life. Take into consideration the following actions to clear the path for the fresh and to let go of the old. Establish personal as well as professional objectives for the near future. Develop an attitude of gratitude to better concentrate on the here and now good. Establish new bonds or work on strengthening interrelations that have the potential to become great friendships; practice mindfulness so you learn how else to return to the present when your brain goes to the past; commit to one conscience activity each month; clean and organize your spaces, so you give away or discard products that no longer serve you; commit to the new hobby or activity each month; establish new connections or try to strengthen causal connections that have the potential to be a special bond

5. Prioritizing Yourself May Help

Putting yourself first requires making deliberate choices in all aspects of your life. It could begin with the realization that choosing what is beneficial for oneself does not equate to acting in a self-centered manner. Putting the self-first may mean regaining your power by focusing on healing in the here and now rather than dwelling on what has caused you pain in the past. It should be about coming to terms with the fact that you matter. Consider the following:

- going to therapy to try to discover how to let go of the past & the hurt you've experienced;
- setting limitations with other people that might want to recall or discuss the past when you're not ready to;
- making life decisions that cause you to feel safe, at peace, or happy, even if you don't agree;
- reframing thoughts which might increase your anxiety or sadness to fixate on thoughts that may make you feel hopeful;
- making life choices that make you feel safe, at peace, or happy; making life decisions that practice self-kindness and respect for oneself in daily life.

Putting yourself first could also mean looking into different avenues where you might find forgiveness. Researchers have found that being able to forgive oneself and others is related to higher psychological well-being levels. It includes having a stronger tolerance for uncertainty and a lesser tendency to feel angry.

6. Lessons

What have you discovered about life, yourself, relationships, and love due to the painful experiences you've had in the past? Your initial reaction to this inquiry might be to consider the unfavorable things you've picked up along the way. It makes sense and has merit. But try to pause when this is your initial response and think about how you may instead concentrate on a few valuable lessons. For instance, the things you now know you don't want in your life, the coping skills individuals may have developed to deal with life's challenges, the sense everything that passes and that this, too, shall pass, how strong and resilient you may be, who showed up in your life and proved you could rely on them, the things you now know you don't want in your life, and so on. Is there a "WHY" that justifies the things that they do? More significantly, are you living the life that you have deliberately chosen for yourself, one that you have crafted of your own volition based on the tastes and aspirations that are uniquely yours? The answer to this problem is "no," and it is a resounding "no" for most men in today's world. Since birth, the typical man has always chosen the course of action that offers the fewest obstacles to overcome. The most unforgettable times in his life were spent throughout his youth, specifically his childhood and adolescence. By the stage he enters the workforce and reaches the age of 30, he has pretty much provided up on the idea of exploring fresh experiences in his life. He doesn't seem interested in furthering his development or achieving more in life; rather, he seems to live in an atmosphere of scorn and anger. Because it was either his first job or the only employment that was provided to him, he spends most of his work, especially in such a cell that he finds intolerable. Given that she was a former classmate and dropped into his lap, he chooses to date or marries a female who isn't particularly attractive to him but does so out of convenience. Or perhaps he is unattached and lives alone. A small percentage of guys are fortunate enough to have built for themselves the kind of life they take great pleasure in leading. The job for themselves or in a job they purposefully choose, and they date multiple women at the same time or just one person who they are genuinely attracted to and who contributes real value to their life. On the other hand, these guys are an anomaly. They merely account for an exceedingly small portion of the total population. The downfall of the typical contemporary guy may be seen everywhere. He is sliding farther and further away from being the self-reliant and self-assured adventurer and coming closer and closer to being the polite recluse who is satisfied with his everyday life. You have now entered the age of weakness. Gentlemen, you have arrived in the era of weakness, in which it is uncommon to go after what you want but also frowned upon by the majority, who are envious of those who do so. Welcome to this age. They despise that someone else might be able to break from the constraints that have kept them from transforming their lives or finding a life that is more in line with what they desire, particularly if it is a friend or a close acquaintance of theirs. It just serves as a reminder to them of the worries and uncertainties that they have within themselves - the ones they don't dare to face. I must pause here and ask everyone the relevant points because we've reached this point: Are you going to be slowed down? Will you give in to the pressure to conform to today's increasingly standard way of living? Or are you setting yourself free and genuinely putting in the effort to build the life you want? When will you stop being just another dumb freak who lives and reacts? Aggressive behavior is the only strategy that will allow you to escape this cycle of self-destructive behavior. You must actively and aggressively take control of your life until you discover a way out, or even better until they find a method to make your path out.

2.1: You Cannot Attend For The Proper Time To Come Along

You can't keep waiting for everything to fall into place exactly right. You also can't wait for another person's hand to pull them out of the situation. You begin life alone, and you end it alone as well. At the finish of the day, there is no one else but yourself on which you can rely. It would be best if you molded yourself into a guy who rules over life. If you don't change your ways, you'll end up following the standard route, which leads to being controlled by life.

Take, for instance, the fact that the dominating male possesses a social presence that cannot be ignored. His aggressive attitude to understanding what he wants and attaining it expresses an overbearing sense of confidence because of how he goes about it. He exudes confidence, flashes a warm smile, and makes direct eye contact with you while he unflinchingly relays the required information. The typical Joe has a disposition that can be described as apprehensive or reserved.

It is a direct outcome of the numerous deep-seated fears he continuously brings with him everywhere he goes. Because he cannot articulate his goals, he lives in perpetual anxiety. So, are you in control of your life, or have you allowed yourself to become a victim of simply living and counting down the days until you pass away?

How To Avoid Feeling Regret In The Years To Come

You need to be offensive and defensive like any excellent sports team if you genuinely want to be free by hand from the chains of regret. Only then will you be competent to truly set yourself free. Examine your internal state to strengthen your defensive strategy. Take note of what you are thinking. Evaluate your emotions. What kinds of judgments go through your head when you experience different feelings, and how true are those thoughts? Then it would help if you took the offensive. Put your thoughts into action or find evidence to support, refute, or amend them. Consider how your life may be altered if you discover that a certain belief is incorrect.

One of Dr. Hooper's favorite mantras is embodied in this offensive and defensive strategy: "When I believe it, I behave towards something, and eventually, I become it." You will always behave in a way directed toward your regret, and you will eventually become it if you do not take a defensive attitude against your bad, toxic thoughts of regret. Purifying and elucidating your worldview won't occur in a single sitting or even in a single day. It's not a stroll in the green at all! It would help if you dismantled your previous beliefs before advancing in a different route supported by your new beliefs. The trouble with views is that you think they are true, which is the problem! Because of this, the process of auditing is quite significant. If you adjust your beliefs, you will change how you think; ultimately, your life will change. Intentionally live your life. Dr. Hooper's incredibly astute words remind us that each of us needs to be deliberate about the kind of life we need to lead. It's not something that happens by chance!

The procedure is far less complicated than you might imagine:

The first step is to visualize reaching your goal line one day at a time.

The second step is to break these larger goals into more manageable chunks. For instance, if you wish to start each morning with mindfulness at 6:00 AM and value meditating for the depth it brings, then set your alarms for 5:45 AM. These seemingly insignificant, purposeful adjustments to one's behavior can lead to extraordinary advances when carried out repeatedly.

Your relationship with oneself, just like a marriage, develops over time through an unlimited number of seemingly insignificant interactions and exchanges. Even successful people have failures and things they wish they could change. In the end, we're only human. These approaches can potentially steer us toward the correct path when addressing chronic problems and open wounds. These last comments from Dr. Hooper do a fantastic job of encapsulating this message. "While battling regret, utilize it as a time for your heart and brain to open to a new perspective. This perspective is actually about connectivity — connectedness to God, connectedness to yourself, and connectedness to the rest of creation."

2.2: Activities that can help with anxiety

Anxiety is a natural response that humans have while under pressure. However, having excessive anxiety might prevent one from enjoying a healthy and happy life. If you feel your worry is consuming you, you can find comfort by performing any of the exercises listed below whenever and whenever you want. These exercises aim to help you relax in a hurry through physical activity.

1. Take Some Deep Breaths To Relax

When experiencing anxiety, you may become aware that your heart rate and respiration have accelerated. You may also start to sweat and have feelings of lightheadedness or dizziness. When you're feeling worried, gaining control of your breathing can help simultaneously relax both body and mind. Take a deep breath & follow these techniques to bring your breathing back under control when you're feeling anxious: Sit in a calm and pleasant spot. Place one hand on your chest and another on your stomach as you do this exercise. When you take a full breath, you should feel more movement in your stomach than in your chest. Please take a thick breath out of your nose and try to keep it slow and steady. Observe and become aware of your hands as you take a breath in. The hand on your stomach should move very slightly, while the hand on your chest would remain immobile. Take a few thick breaths in and out through

39

your lips. Repeat this practice at least ten times or until your anxiety begins to ease.

2. Put Your Mind At Ease By Envisioning

Have you ever come across the expression "finding your happy place"? Creating an icon in your brain of a setting that creates a sense of tranquility can have a calming influence on your brain and your body. If you are beginning to feel anxious, choose a calm and relaxing spot to sit in. Imagine the perfect environment for you to unwind in. It doesn't matter where in the globe it is or if it's real or imagined; the important thing is that the image brings you feelings of serenity, happiness, peace, and security. Make sure it is not too tough to think about so you may bring it back into your thoughts when you feel nervous. Imagine all the minute particulars you would notice when you were there. Consider what the environment would be like to smell, touch, and hear. Imagine that you are already there and relaxing and having fun. When you have a clear emotional image of your "happy spot," close your eyes and concentrate on breathing normally and slowly through your nose while exhaling through your mouth. Do this for a few minutes. Be conscious of your breaths and keep your attention fixed on the location you've conjured up in your mind if it takes to experience a reduction in your anxiety. Return to this mental location if you find yourself becoming nervous.

3. Relax Your Muscles

It's common to feel tense or strained in the muscles when worried feelings take over your body. The muscle tension can make it more difficult to cope with your worry when you feel it. In most cases, you may lower your anxiety levels by reducing the stress that has built up in your muscles. In times of high anxiety, the following can help you swiftly relieve muscle tension: Sit in a calm and pleasant spot. Turn your attention to your breath while you close your eyes. Take a few/some deep breaths, inhaling out of your nose & exhaling through your mouth. Raise a tight fist with the hand you're using. Make a tight fist with your hand. Maintain the clenched fist position for a few moments. Take note of the tension that is building up in your hand. Open your fingers slowly while remaining conscious of how they feel. You may become aware of a release of tension in your hand. Your hand will eventually feel less weighted and more relaxed as time goes on. Repeat the process of contracting and then relaxing the various muscular endurance in your spine, starting with your hands, and working your way down to your feet and shoulders. You might find it helpful to move around and up your body while tensing different sets of muscles as you do so. It would help if you

41

refrained from tensing the tissues in any part of your body that is hurting or wounded because doing so can worsen your injury.

4. Calm Down

You can easily reduce the stress and worry you feel by counting. Find a peaceful and cozy spot to sit down and take a few deep breaths whenever you feel anxious. Put your hand over your eyes and count to 10 very slowly. If that doesn't work, keep going until you reach 20 or even greater. Continue counting until you see a decrease in the level of anxiety you're feeling. The relief may come on suddenly, while at other times, it may not come for some time. Keep your cool and be patient. Counting can help you relax since it provides you with something else to concentrate on aside from the anxiousness that you are feeling. It is an excellent technique to utilize in a crowded or bustling location, such as a store or train, when other anxiety exercises could be tougher.

Chapter 3: Healing and Anger Management Techniques

"Let us not look back in anger, nor forward in fear, but around in awareness."– James Thurber

It is normal and beneficial to feel angry sometimes. However, it may manifest in a manner that is disproportionate to the cause of it. In situations like these, the feeling may hamper a person's decision-making ability, damage relationships, and inflict other harm. The emotional harm may be mitigated by developing better control over one's emotions.

The emotion of anger is a typical reaction for people who are faced with a difficult or dangerous situation. It's also a secondary reaction to negative emotions like loneliness, fear, or melancholy. In some circumstances, the feeling may materialize out of thin air. A person's relationships, psychological well-being, and overall quality of life may all be negatively impacted when anger is experienced often and excessively. A detrimental and long-lasting effect may also be produced by repressing and bottling up one's emotions.

People may be helped to come to terms with the sources of their anger and react to these emotions more healthily by using tools and practices. In this book, we discuss both the therapeutic choices that are accessible and the measures that a person may do at home to help themselves.

3.1: Therapy

Group or individual counseling may be useful in learning to recognize and cope with problematic behaviors. Examples of why a person could benefit from seeing a doctor or other medical expert are:

- Getting in trouble with the law frequently
- Having intense assertions with family, friends, or coworkers
- Frequently getting into fights and physical confrontations
- Regularly violently attacking a partner or child
- Threatening violence to folks or property
- Breaking artifacts during an outburst
- Losing their cool when driving & becoming reckless

There is usually additional than one contributing factor to an anger problem. The following are some of the mental health conditions from which they may stem

- Addiction to drugs or alcohol
- A disease of manic-depressive swings
- Schizophrenia and other schizotypal personality disorders
- Psychiatric Illnesses
- Disturbances in the borderline personality

Disproportionate rage may be mitigated by addressing the underlying causes. However, there are occasions when one must learn to master rage independently. Getting management therapy in either group or private sessions with a therapist is possible. Individuals' anger management strategies should be informed by any psychiatric diagnoses they may have acquired. Anger management classes teach their students how to

- Find the causes
- Positive actions in the face of anger or prevention by addressing causes
- Moderating excessive and illogical thinking
- Bring yourself back to a height of serenity, even if you're in a tense situation; say what you need and how you feel in a forceful but not aggressive way, and then focus your attention and efforts on finding a solution.

If you're in therapy or counseling, a good therapist or counselor will help you work through these issues

- Can you tell me the signs of anger?
- Who are the individuals, what are the events, where do they take place, and what other factors contribute to my anger?
- When I feel anger rising, what should I do? Can you tell me what to do?
- To what extent do other people feel the effects of my anger?

The realization that rage and tranquility are not binary states might be helpful. For instance, anger might start as moderate annoyance and escalate into full-blown wrath. Understanding the range may help individuals distinguish between genuine anger and exaggerated responses to trivial triggers. Helping patients recognize and use these differences is a primary goal of treatment.

3.2 Keep an angry journal

People may find it easier to predict triggers and find healthier ways to manage anger if they keep a journal of their emotions of anger during an episode & detail what occurred before, during, and after the event. Learning which methods of self-control were successful and which were not might assist a person in developing a more effective strategy for anger management. It is important to acknowledge and not suppress the sentiments that led to the rage. Instead, after you have gained your composure, you should communicate with them in an authoritative but not aggressive manner. Keeping a diary might be a useful outlet for accomplishing this goal.

Writing may also assist a person in recognizing ideas that lead to excessive rage and assisting them in changing such thoughts. The transformation of catastrophic or conclusive thinking processes into more grounded and productive ones may greatly assist. For instance, replacing the thinking that "everything is wrecked" with the thought that "this is frustrating, but just a resolution is available" might help clarify the issue and enhance the likelihood that a solution can be found.

3.3: Anger Management in Tense Situations

A person may help relieve their emotions and think about potential solutions by taking a brief stroll. When facing individuals about certain issues, scenarios, or complaints, anger may surface for no apparent reason. The ability to confront these issues constructively may help mitigate the effects of anger and contribute to resolving the underlying cause. It may be useful in

- A person in the throes of excessive or unreasonable rage may find it difficult to believe that a situation will improve if they hear phrases such as "always" or "never," hence it is important to avoid such terms.
- Let go of your resentment since holding onto it will only feed your anger and make it more difficult to manage.
- Good-natured humor, on the other hand, may assist soothe anger and resentment, so try to avoid cutting or caustic comedy.

- Timing is essential; if conversations in the evening often degenerate into shouting matches, for instance, because people are very sleepy, switching up when these conversations occur is a good idea.
- Working toward a compromise may help everyone involved experience more good feelings if done constructively.

Symptoms

As a person progresses from a state of moderate annoyance to one of wrath, they could feel the following

- Need to get away from the predicament
- Irritation, melancholy, or depression
- Guilt \resentment \anxiety
- Need to strike out, either verbally or violently, with force

There is also a possibility of the following bodily manifestations taking place

- Rubbing the face with a hand, fidgeting, or
- clutching one hand with the other
- pacing around
- becoming cynical, rude, rude, or abrasive
- losing their sense of humor
- craving substances that a person believes will instill a sense

of calm, such as liquor, tobacco, or drugs raising vocal volume or pitch screaming or crying, losing their sense of humor

Additionally, a person may experience the following

- An uncomfortable feeling in the stomach
- A racing heart rate
- Quick, shallow breathing
- Hot flashes inside the face or neck,
- Shaking hands, lips, or jaws
- Tingling in the back of the neck

If a person seems to be able to detect acute pain or fury in the present time, they can apply management strategies to gain control of the situation.

Chapter 4: Practicing Self-love and Improving Self-esteem

"Seek to be whole, not perfect."– Oprah

As someone committed to assisting others in enhancing their well-being and fostering their development, one of the questions that often crosses my mind is this: how do you urge someone to change? The simple response is that individuals can only change once they are prepared to do so. But this raises a new question: at what point are individuals ready to alter their behaviors?

There's the possibility of falling into a trap inside any self-help instruction. You must believe that you are deserving of improvements. If you have poor self-esteem, the only way to establish value is by active participation in life's experiences. This paradox exemplifies the maturation process: how can a person cultivate self-love while having a poor opinion of themselves?

To our relief, a route leads away from this seeming impasse. In this piece, I'll walk you through ways to fall in love with yourself. I'm going to go through some of how you could become stuck, as well as the most effective strategy to increase your sense of self-worth and the most important connection to you in your life: your relationship with yourself.

4.1: What is self-esteem?

Do you criticize your actions or words to yourself? Do you fear making a mistake? Relax. You aren't awful and probably get at least one task very well. Maybe it's time to give your self-esteem a tune-up. According to Yale University experts, having a "poor hair day" might harm your emotional well-being. What would happen if you were late for work if something as little as an unruly coif could "diminish your self-esteem and generate emotions of ineptitude, self-doubt, and even self-hatred"? Have you ever fought with your boss?

All aspects of our lives are inspired by how we think about ourselves. To overcome obstacles and pursue satisfaction, one must feel good.

There is a range of levels of self-esteem. A lack of self-confidence, harsh judgments about one's abilities, and an overall bad feeling about one's value are all indicators of low self-esteem. Accepting praises or remarks on the positive aspects of your character might be challenging at times. Even if we all experience mild insecurity, low self-esteem only becomes a problem when it causes significant disruptions in one's day-to-day existence.

Esteem is located towards the peak of the pyramid in Abraham Maslow's theory of the Hierarchy of Needs, right below the self-actualization level. According to Maslow's theory, one of the most crucial factors in flourishing as a human being is esteem. He divided the concept of esteem into two distinct subheadings: respect for oneself and the desire to garner regard from other people.

Comparison is often the source of low self-esteem due to the connection between how we see ourselves and how we evaluate the qualities of others. People with a low sense of self-worth are more inclined to compare themselves negatively to others, which may lead to a downward cycle of even lower self-worth.

4.2: Foundation of Self-esteem

A feeling of self-worth is synonymous with self-esteem. What you think concerning yourself and whether you regard yourself. It may involve how you feel regarding your conduct, abilities, IQ, or emotions and how you see your physical appearance. The concept of one's worth develops and changes throughout time. It is formed by the person and the people in their environment. Some of the followings are examples of factors that might affect self-esteem:

- A familial environment that is hostile, abusive, or inattentive may contribute to poor self-esteem.

- A healthy and loving home environment may contribute to improved levels of self-esteem.

- Bullying, social isolation, and difficulties fitting in with peers are common at school or work.

- Illnesses caused by medicine, particularly those that place restrictions on one's body or mind

- Patterns of thought and characteristics of personality

- Issues relating to one's mental health, such as sadness or anxiety

- The role of genetics in determining how the brain grows and functions

The foundation of our self-esteem is laid throughout childhood, yet it is malleable and subject to change throughout our lives. We must keep an eye out for times when our self-esteem is lower than usual and remember that we already have the power to shift it back to a good state.

Positive self-esteem

People who have a healthy sense of their worth have attributes such as the following:

- Capacity to speak their minds, convey their beliefs, and communicate their requirements, ideas, and thoughts.

- Feel at ease while responding with "no."

- They are conscious of their capabilities and accepting of

both their talents and flaws, even if they're attempting to improve themselves.

- Stronger and more equipped to bounce back from adverse experiences or circumstances and able to maintain relationships, whether romantic and otherwise, based on love and respect

- Appreciate oneself as well as the other people around them.

- Don't dwell on the past or beat yourself up over errors you made in the past.

- Accept the difficulties, and when you inevitably fail, learn from your errors.

Low self-esteem

Your feeling of well-being might be negatively impacted by having low or negative self-esteem. It can alienate you from your thoughts, emotions, and requirements. In addition, it reduces your capacity to make decisions that benefit your health in love, work, and leisure. A low sense of self-worth may result in the following:

- Overachievers, perfectionists, and control freaks sometimes have the misconception that they must attain a certain level of success before you can love them, rather than just being loved for who they are.

- A persistent dread of being abandoned, which may lead to difficulties in relationships

- Difficulty making choices because of the fear that doing so may result in losing affection or respect for oneself or another.

- Examples of avoidance behaviors include consuming excessive amounts of food, smoking, abusing alcohol or drugs, or engaging in obsessive shopping to escape unpleasant emotions of alienation, anxiety, or self-loathing.

- Having difficulty with taking compliments

- Negative self-talk as well as assuming that there is no middle ground, "Because I did not do well in this one endeavor, people should consider me a failure in everything,"

Leaning to the Positive

It seems strange that changing your way of thinking might help with low self-esteem. Each person's specific stages will appear different. Think about the following to improve self-esteem:

Be mindful of your negative mental processes. It involves solely focusing on the bad, drawing unfavorable inferences, turning a good thing into a bad one, or undervaluing yourself by saying things like "I do not even deserve better." Check to discover whether you are evaluating yourself based only on feelings or facts by taking a step back. You may break these habits through awareness and replace unhealthy ideas with better ones.

Recognize any factors that might be causing low self-esteem. It may be problems from your youth, present relationships, or the workplace. Understanding where the negativity came from may help you more effectively handle it.

Positive and factual ideas should take the place of negative ones. Examples:

- Realize that everyone makes errors rather than beating yourself up over them. Look for lessons you've picked that will come in handy next time.

- Motivate yourself. Even if it is difficult, I can manage.

- Refrain from making irrational requests like "you must" do anything.

- Use your negative thinking as a cue to talk to yourself positively. It could assist you in replacing negative thinking patterns with positive ones.

- If you are having trouble adjusting, consider therapy. They may help you understand the potential causes of negative thoughts. There are several varieties of treatment. To determine which could be best for you, speak with counselors.

One treatment that helps you recognize negative ideas and then detach yourself from them is acceptance and commitment therapy. Instead of substituting or feeling overpowered by negative thoughts, it tries to reduce their influence.

Some people could erroneously think that improving one's performance, becoming in shape, or increasing one's income would cure their self-esteem. Regardless of any progress, negative thinking patterns will persist. Reality is irrelevant to someone with low self-esteem. These actions might be helpful:

- Ensure your well-being. Pick nutritious meals and work out most days of each week. You'll be in a more positive mood to take better care of yourself if you're feeling well.

- Find activities you like to do. Creating a schedule for a hobby, a spa day, or a visit with friends may be the solution.

- Be mindful of the individuals you spend time with. Avoid those who treat you poorly.

4.3: What exactly does self-love mean?

Self-love is a sentiment in which a person feels affection, affinity, and good self-esteem. There is a strong connection between it and having compassion for oneself. When you have a robust sense of self-love, you are aware of the value you bring to the world and behave in a caring manner toward yourself.

Self-love is a healthy characteristic, in contrast to narcissism, which is characterized by an unhealthy preoccupation with one's thoughts and interests. To love oneself, you need to have a solid comprehension of both your strong points and your problematic areas. In most cases, individuals who suffer from narcissism also have issues with their mental health. But having a healthy love for oneself benefits one's physical health, mental fitness, and interpersonal connections.

Why is it so crucial to love oneself?

Loving oneself is one of the most important things we can do for our overall health. And to what many who strive for perfection may believe, loving oneself does not imply that you do not have high expectations for yourself. It may be difficult to be motivated if we do not have a good attitude about ourselves. According to the findings of several studies, we require self-love to be willing to act, take risks, and pursue new possibilities.

Self-love enables us to take better care of ourselves, experience less stress, and work harder to achieve our goals. However, this also shields us from bad ideas, acts of self-sabotage, and the risk of going beyond our limits. It is essential to acknowledge that being able to say "no" to some things is just as crucial as learning when and how to say "yes" to certain things.

4.4: Activities to improve Self-esteem and Self-love

Everyone has the right to have a positive view of themselves and to take pleasure in their accomplishments; fortunately, healthy self-esteem is within everyone's reach. Here are seven actions that can help you build your self-esteem and bring you closer to your goal.

1. Every day, educate yourself on something new.

We naturally tend to concentrate less on failing and making

errors when we shift our attention toward learning and progressing. Take, for the occasion, the scenario in which you have finished a workpiece and your supervisor hands it back to you with some input to assist you in improving it. You have the option of being hard on yourself and being critical of yourself for not having it right from the beginning, or you can focus on learning from the comments and considering things for the future.

The more we become accustomed to learning, developing, and trying something new (while being willing to receive constructive criticism), the more we tend to feel as if we are making progress in life, and the less we feel like our comfort bubble constrains us.

Learning new skills not only helps us boost our self-esteem and conviction, but it may also make us much more resilient whenever things don't go our way. It is because we can better find meaning in our errors and failings when we have more knowledge to draw on.

The following is a list of enjoyable and uncomplicated methods by which you might acquire new knowledge:

- Listen to podcasts

- Becoming involved in a new artistic endeavor or pastime.

- Be available to read literature on personal development and empowerment.

- Attend a lecture or hands-on sessions such as photography, meditation, pottery, or cooking

- Enroll in one online course.

- Communicate with a variety of individuals and experience new environments.

- Start new employment or become a volunteer.

- read blogs

2. Create a notebook with the heading "Strengths and Achievements."

Spend some time before the end of every day thinking about the things you did well that day, no matter how large or little they may have been, and all the many ways you put your abilities to use. This activity will enable you to concentrate more on all the nice things you do and the wonderful qualities about yourself rather than getting caught up in just about any negative thoughts that might adversely affect your self-esteem.

Some examples of accomplishments include:

- sticking with your work sometimes when you are tired

- making a great meal from scratch;

- getting out of bed early

- working out for twenty minutes

- complimenting a friend and making them smile

- If you're thirsty, have a water glass rather than a can of soda.

- meditation first thing each morning rather than wasting time on Instagram

Furthermore, some instances of strengths include the following:

1. **Assertiveness**: telling your supervisor you needed so much time on a venture instead of staying up late to get it finished.

2. **Patience**: waiting patiently for your coffee, recognizing that it was a busy few day for the barista.

3. **Kindness**: provide some encouraging comments on their Instagram posts.

4. **Enthusiasm**: Get excited about preparing food a new recipe

5. **Creativity**: Take some beautiful photos of the flowers outside

6. **Confidence**: Start a conversation with a new coworker

3. Give importance to your requirements and care for yourself

Taking good care of yourself and doing pleasant things for

64

yourself are great ways to boost your feeling of the value you bring to the world. You deserve it! You should treat yourself by going out for coffee, getting a massage, relaxing bath, reading a book, or seeing a movie you like. Make it a routine to give importance to your requirements and to the things you do for your self-care.

4. Consistently make attainable sub-goals for yourself

Have you ever aimed for lofty and exciting objectives, only to find that you could not accomplish them since they were beyond your reach? Instead of feeling disappointed and discouraged when you don't reach huge objectives, you may establish a sense of achievement and self-belief by setting modest goals that are important and practical and completing them regularly. It will help you understand/feel more in control of your life.

Imagine, for instance, that you have the objective of running a marathon but haven't trained for a long-distance race in many years. The more time it takes to build up to running marathon distances, the more like a failure you feel and the more inclined you are to quit trying to get there.

On the other hand, if you begin with the objective of running 500 meters and gradually increase it to 1 kilometer, then 1.5 kilometers, and so on, you will have a larger feeling of accomplishment and have a higher opinion of yourself.

5. Stop comparing your everyday existence with the best moments of other people's lives.

Remind yourself that everyone has a life outside of social media, especially if you feel inadequate due to other people's successes, pleasant moments, or life events they have shared on social media. You are often only privy to the positives of other people's lives, and as a result, it is simple to forget that everybody goes through struggles, has obstacles, is flawed, and is susceptible to being hurt.

Take a vacation from social media or spend some time participating in activities that promote self-care if you're finding that everyone else's highlight reels are causing you to feel anxious or overwhelmed.

It is also helpful to donate your time to assist people or animals who are less privileged than you are. It puts things in perspective and tells us that there are greater issues than the inability to get the ideal shot to post on Instagram.

6. Find enjoyable activities to get active.

According to Debbie Mandel, who authored the book "Addicted to Stress," exercising develops mental and physical empowerment. Numerous studies confirm this theory. According to the findings of research that they conducted in 2016, the amount of physical exercise a person performed affected their self-esteem. The study included 300 persons who were aged between the age of 20 and 60 years old. A meta-analysis conducted in 2015 and published in the same year concluded that children and teens who engage in physical exercise experience improvements in their feelings of self-worth and self-confidence.

Exercising your body is an easy method to enhance your self-esteem, and there are numerous activities that you can perform to accomplish this goal while still having a good time.

The following is a list of some of my favorite physically demanding activities:

- Gardening. You will grow physically active as you move

about, bend down, dig, and pluck weeds out of the ground.

- Dog walking. Bring your pets with you, & stroll in the nearby park. Enjoy spending time in the fresh air and playing with the dogs.

- Activities that include water. If the temperature is too high for exercising, you may choose one of the activities that involve water instead. Go swimming, moisture, surfing, hold watersports, kayaking, or snorkeling.

- Waterfall hunting. Who doesn't get excited about concluding a hike to see a breathtaking waterfall? Use Google to compile a list of all the waterfalls you'll be able to see in the area, and then take advantage of any chance you must go waterfall hunting.

- If you want to start moving while you're at home, use an app. You may become in shape by consulting with fitness specialists and engaging in activities such as yoga, tai chi, counting your steps, attempting routines that just need your body weight, or lifting weights.

7. Cultivate greater thankfulness in your life

Building up your self-worth and self-assurance may be facilitated by cultivating a more positive outlook on life. Increasing the amount of appreciation, you feel in your life is one easy approach. And you may go about doing it in several different amusing ways.

- Begin keeping a thankfulness diary by recording at least three things that you are thankful for daily.

- When you gaze in the mirror, give yourself some positive feedback.

- When things don't go as planned, try to find the positive in the situation and express gratitude for it.

- To get your gratitude journal off the ground, start by jotting down one item you're thankful for daily, folding it up, and putting it in a jar. Read all the notes that are in your appreciation jar if you find yourself feeling down, disoriented, or anxious.

- Make use of an affirmation of thankfulness, such as "I am glad for my well-being and happiness," "I am thankful for all the beautiful people I have here in my life," or simply "I feel grateful every single day."

8. Start a self-esteem wishlist

wish list

It is essential to put in the effort to carry out activities that might increase one's sense of self-worth. Reading about ways to improve your self-esteem might make it easy to forget about putting such strategies into practice in your day-to-day existence. Make a list for yourself, and then take some time to sit down and think about the numerous things you can do to help foster confidence and self-worth. Here is an illustration to serve as a starting point for you.

Daily Exercises to Boost One's Self-Esteem

- Write in a journal or diary.

- Take note of my many accomplishments and qualities

- Engage in some type of physical exercise for twenty minutes.

- Pay attention to my hygiene and dress in a way that boosts my confidence.

- Expand your knowledge by reading one chapter from a

book on how to assist yourself.

Self-Esteem Building Exercises every week.

- Confront an arduous task or difficult difficulty that I've been putting off.

- Spend quality time with a person who inspires and encourages me.

- Think back on what I've picked up and figure out how I can become better/grow.

- Devote some of your moment/time each day to meaningful acts of self-care.

Chapter 5: How Not To Be Influenced By Negative Thoughts And Feelings

"Deal with your negative patterns before they become habits because habits are hard to break."— Germany Kent

Negative thought shapes/patterns, also known as cognitive distortions, can result in false assumptions, exaggerated self-criticisms, and even outright rejection of reality. However, the ramifications of this line of thought might be too real for someone who is already battling with their mental health.

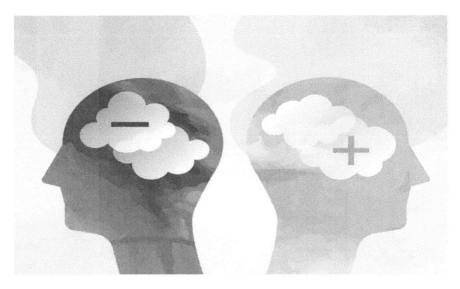

Learning how to successfully cope with the emotions and emotions that lead to bad thinking is needed to break the cycle of pessimism that keep one stuck in a negative thought loop. A person having difficulties with their mental health may be led into a depressive circular pattern of bad thoughts by any one of several possible triggers. These triggers may range from giving unhelpful advice to having minor relationship problems, and the negative thoughts themselves may take various forms. Several hypotheses attempt to explain why human beings often appear so fixated on the unfavorable parts of existence. Struggle and conflict are frequently elevated to heroic status in our culture and the media. The drive to fight and stay alive is ingrained in our genetic makeup because of evolution. Even the most recent chapters in human history are often filled with bloodshed and terrifying events. It is maybe not surprising that we might become so preoccupied with the unfavorable aspects of our surroundings. What do you believe is the primary reason for negative thinking? Because negative thinking stems from a complex network of interconnected and ever-changing circumstances, there isn't a single primary reason we can point to its origin. The major driver of a pattern of negative thought will differ widely based on the person engaging in the pattern of negative thinking, their specific history, the triggers, and their present state of mental health. Whatever the underlying cause of our negative thinking patterns, we can take actions that will empower us to conquer them and free ourselves from their effect. Negative thinking develops into a larger pattern, an example of cognitive distortion.

When potentially destructive thought patterns recur repeatedly, we have a situation that fits the description of a grandiose delusion. The term "distortion" is employed since these negative ideas lead to either incorrect or unrealistic conclusions or even a distortion of reality itself. Cognitive distortions, to put it in such terms, are inaccuracies in thinking. To be more precise, the phrase refers to a way of thinking that can be self-destructive, nihilistic, or insecure, and that causes people to have damaging false beliefs about themselves and their role in the world. It can produce or aggravate mental health issues such as anxiety and depression. The ability to recognize cognitive distortions is a necessary step in overcoming their influence. You have a bigger chance of breaking the negative thinking pattern before it escalates into a major mental health crisis if you recognize the issue when it is first beginning and find a way to deal with it. Believing that you are undeserving of love or prosperity, believing that everyone hates you, feeling yourself for your parents' divorce, and holding other self-destructive ideas are all common cognitive distortions. The self-deprecating nature of cognitive errors is not always the case, though. They also can be projected on with other individuals and the environment around you, such as believing that everyone around you is lying, blaming another individual or institution for their issues, or becoming obsessed with a partner's sentiments toward you.

5.1: The Relationship Between Unhealthy Thought Patterns and Major Depressive Disorder

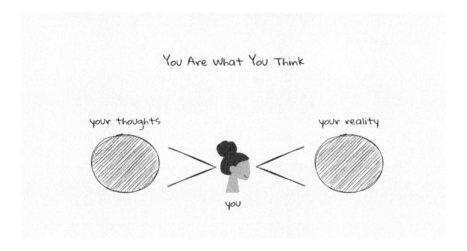

Anyone who has ever struggled with depression will find that the connection between depressive thinking patterns and negative thought patterns is not surprising. The relationship between them is circular and, in a sense, like the chicken-and-egg problem, almost paradoxical. Is having a pessimistic outlook one of the symptoms of depression? Yes, but the converse is also true: negative thinking can contribute to depression. Even on a good day, a person who suffers from clinical depression may find it difficult to muster the will to drag themselves out of bed and face the day. When you combine this factor with a negative mindset that leads to just a feeling of hopelessness (for example, "What's the point of not getting out of bed even if nobody cares about me?"), you have another big hurdle that impairs the depressed person's capacity to function, even less heal.

1. Polarization

It occurs when complicated situations are oversimplified to the point where they turn into black or white, yea or no, good vs. bad (or me or them) matters. Because of this all-or-nothing mentality, it is difficult to approach problems in a way that allows for any complexity or possibility for compromise. A typical and potentially destructive example of dichotomous thinking is the belief that "there is no second place," which means that to be successful, one must be the absolute best at what one does.

2. Emotional Reasoning

Individuals engage in emotional rhetoric when they insist that a situation is factually correct, even though their only proof is their feelings. Because they base their reasoning on unpleasant feelings rather than logic, it is impossible to have a fruitful conversation with someone in the throes of emotional reasoning. The emotionally rational person begins by assuming that their bad sentiments must be true and legitimate simply because they exist and then develops a narrative to back up this assertion to demonstrate that the premise is true. An example of emotion-driven reasoning is, "Because I get nervous about being at school, it follows that going to class must be risky."

3. Overgeneralization

Concentrating on a single unfavorable aspect of your life or experience and attributing an inflated level of significance to it is an example of overgeneralization. For instance, when clearing the table, a waiter accidentally breaks a glass, which prompts them to proclaim, "I'm the most inept waiter in the history of the world!" This hopeless outlook is disproportionate to the occurrence that sparked it in the first place. Someone could arrive at such a conclusion if they overgeneralized the person's entire career and placed it in the perspective of this insignificant error.

4. Labeling

Another prevalent sort of destructive way of thought that many individuals engage in daily without quite thinking about it is assigning negative labels to themselves and the places and events in their immediate environment. If someone has a persistent negative perception of themselves, such as "a loser," "stupid," or "a bad father," it is possible that they will eventually conform to that image. Their pessimistic outlook does not allow them any space to live outside of those labels or develop beyond them.

5. Leaping to Conclusions

Most of us have been accountable for making an incorrect assumption at some point. If, on the other hand, a person struggling with their mental health jumps to a hasty conclusion about everything — it can become incredibly difficult to erase or change that perception.

6. Mental Filtering

It is when a person decides (either consciously or unconsciously) to memorize only the negative aspects of a scenario. It is an example of mental filtering. A depressed footballer who neglects their many outstanding plays and screams about one blown assignment and how it won their team the game is an example of conceptual filtering.

7. Telling fortune

It is an example of a negative thought pattern that entails making repeated predictions that the outcomes of certain circumstances would be unpleasant.

Your negative picture of the future can become so powerful that it interferes with your capacity to behave in a manner that might lead to positive outcomes if you continue to project your pessimism into the future. It is what is known as a self-satisfying prophecy. For instance, a student who has an upcoming test and believes that they will fail may decide not to bother studying for the test, which ultimately results in the student failing it.

8. Reading People's Minds

Predicting the future and being able to read people's minds may seem like extraordinary psychic talents, but when we're talking about cognitive bias, neither of these things is especially helpful. In this sense, "mind reading" refers to the assumption that one knows another person's thoughts and feelings, particularly concerning how they feel about themselves. A negative example of mind-reading behavior would be to assume that someone despises you because they responded to a question with a brief and hasty statement when it's possible that they were merely flustered with something unrelated to the topic at hand.

9. Exaggerating

It is a problem, or making it seem much worse than it is, is something most of us can do when we are angry. Magnification, also known as catastrophizing, merely exaggerates a problem's significance beyond what it is. Catastrophizing would be letting a single unpleasant experience, such as a horrible cab ride, spoil an entire vacation.

10. Wrong

Everyone likes the feeling of being accurate, but this desire can become a cognitive illusion when it takes precedence over evidence, logic, and the material world around them. It is necessary for growth, particularly the kind of growth required for mental health rehabilitation, to give yourself permission to forgive yourself and make room for growth. If there is no possibility that you might ever be wrong from the beginning, there is no room for that evolution to take place.

11. Control Fallacies

A control fallacy has the potential to present itself in two distinct ways. The first reason is that you feel hopeless since you have no authority over anything occurring in your life and seem unable to alter it. The other reason could be that you feel hopeless since you have complete control over every aspect of your life and are, as a result, solely responsible for any unfavorable or challenging circumstances.

12. Fallacies Concerning Fairness

The age-old saying "the world is not fair" is typically said regarding someone having difficulty with an unfairness fallacy. Examining circumstances in terms of how right or unjustly they can be a fruitful exercise from a socio-political standpoint, but it is not always beneficial to one's mental health.

13. Believing

Believing that someone or anything will eventually alter to meet your requirements is a myth of change. Believing or expecting that something will change to suit your needs is also a fallacy of change. You are, in essence, imposing your requirements and preferences on the reality that is immediately surrounding you.

14. Underestimating the significance of something or giving it less weight

Not all negative mind patterns are genuinely concentrated on negative thoughts. It is another type of cognitive distortion when someone fails to recognize the good things happening in their lifetime and instead chooses to dismiss or minimize them. This failure to recognize the good enables the growth of negative feelings that are not inhibited in any way. To minimize your achievements by attributing them entirely to "chance" is a case of depreciation. Personalization and self-blame come hand in hand. Personalization occurs when you take issues and details that have nothing to do with you and make them mostly about yourself, your sentiments, or your role in matters. Self-blame occurs when you take problems or details that have nothing to do with you and make them everything about your role. One of the best common types of personalization is when a child believes they are to blame for breaking up their parent's marriage.

15. Imperatives

Thinking about something in terms such as "should" or "must" can significantly contribute to negative thinking. For instance, a person who suffers from anxiety when talking on the phone may berate herself because they believe they "should" be harshly able to make even the most basic phone call without experiencing any unease. It is more than difficult for them to acknowledge that it's normal to feel nervous, which, in turn, stops them from engaging in the action steps necessary to effectively manage their anxiety. Instead, they continue to waste their time being pointlessly upset over the fact that they are experiencing anxiety. Not every pattern of anxious thoughts will perfectly fit into one of the classifications presented above, and frequently two or so more forms of grandiose delusion will develop simultaneously. In other instances, one form of pessimism will lead to another, so building more intricate routines that could require much hard effort and help to be broken.

5.2: Patterns Of Behavior That Can Cause Cognitive Distortions

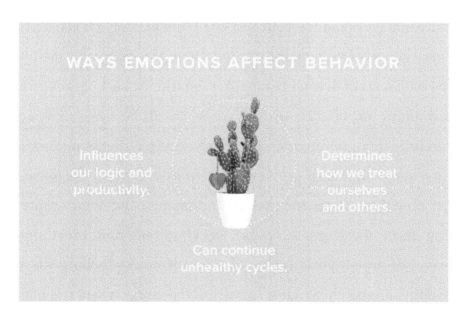

Finding patterns within patterns is an important part of working on improving your mental health. You may be importing into your day-to-day existence certain mental habits and attitudes that lead to cycles of a negative mindset. These attitudes and habits can be broken. You can be of assistance to yourself by acquiring the ability to notice them as they take place and putting a stop to them before they take you to a detrimental position.

Harmful Thought Patterns

One should be thorough before making significant decisions; nevertheless, if you cannot choose where to go for lunchtime because you are beset by uncertainty and doubt, you are engaging in a negative thought pattern. When you overthink a situation, you examine your responsibility in every choice from every conceivable perspective and attempt to mentally model the outcomes of every imaginable scenario. At best, this can be a draining experience, and at worst, it can be tragic if your carefully thought forecasts are utterly incorrect. Set boundaries for your thoughts to prevent them from becoming excessive. Set time constraints for making judgments, and then ensure you meet those goals. Yoga, working out, and breathing exercises are all good options for you if you're looking for a healthy approach to clear some of the unnecessary mental clutter from your head.

Ruminating Self-Reflection And Consciousness

These can be beautiful things; however, negativity and unhappiness can be terrible if your thought process is twisted by negativity and unhappiness. A rumination is a form of meditation. Do you frequently concentrate on shortcomings and blunders rather than considering how things could be improved? Negative rumination is a pattern in and of itself that repeats itself by projecting your shortcomings onto your image of the future, leading you to assume that your lifestyle will only worsen as time goes on. When you become aware that you are fixating on negative ideas, it is time to break the pattern by engaging in a different activity. Never allow yourself to relax with your thoughts. You could try to confuse yourself by taking a book, watching a movie, working on a profession, or visiting a friend, but you shouldn't utilize these activities as a simple outlet for the unpleasant ideas running through your head. Stay away from distractions like food and alcohol. Consuming an excessive amount of food and being drunk can make the problem even worse.

Cynical Hostility

It is a groupthink mentality involving directing wrath, suspicion, judgment, or contempt at others. The following characteristics characterize cynical hostility: These emotions could result from insecurity, exaggeration, or emotional baggage from the past. Because you view other people as intrinsically harmful, bad, or untrustworthy, it is difficult to build a support system when you think this way. Researchers have shown a connection between this antagonistic mood and a higher risk of heart disease and high blood pressure. Use empathy as a weapon against hostile cynicism. Try to look at a matter from every conceivable angle rather than going with your gut instinct to be suspicious. Find methods to reframe challenging circumstances as opportunities for collaboration rather than competition.

Imagine You Are Going Shopping

Visualizing oneself in a supermarket is one of the distraction strategies that Winch recommends using. He instructs us to "Try to envision all of the things on one shelf as in store, and the orientation that you observe them in." You aren't doing a lot of shopping for food, do you? Think of something else that needs your attention, like the order in which the books on the bookshelf are arranged or the order in which the songs are arranged on a lap or playlist that you enjoy listening to. You need to do it for a short period—perhaps thirty seconds or one minute—but the most important thing is to be rigorous about it and perform the action each whenever that negative thinking returns, even if this means acting twenty times in an hour.

Winch says, "It may appear as though it is only momentary, but if you practice these patterns sufficiently, it can improve both your happiness and ability to make decisions." You may retrain your brain to think differently in response to certain triggers, such as when you have certain thoughts.

Maintain Good Spirited Companions

The people in your social circle may have anything to do with why you can't shake those troubling feelings that keep coming back. Researchers from the University of Notre Dame revealed in a study carried out in 2013 that it is rather usual for college learners to pick up tendencies like rumination from their roommates. According to the study, other people easily imitate rumination because it frequently entails worrying and speaking one's thoughts aloud. If possible, avoid people who are always pessimistic, or at the very least, be conscious of how their attitudes could influence your own.

Please Get Rid Of Them In The Traditional Sense

According to research conducted at The Ohio State University in 2012, getting rid of a lingering fear may be as simple as writing it onto a piece of paper and then throwing it away. It could be as simple as that. Individuals who jotted down unpleasant thoughts about their bodies and then started throwing them away maintained a more positive impression of themselves a few minutes ago compared to those who kept the same papers with them.

Those who wrote down the negative things concerning their bodies but then threw those away gained a more positive sense of self. According to Richard Petty, Ph.D., a co-author of the study and a professor of psychology at Stanford University, "How you categorize your thoughts—as worthless or as deserving of protection—seems to have an impact. in how you employ those thoughts." Do you wish to avoid wasting paper? This activity could also be completed on the computer by dragging textual data into the "trash can." This method was also successful.

Have A Snack

Negative thoughts can arise from various factors; nevertheless, if you notice that you are preoccupied with isolation, you could find that physically warming up relieves you. In a study conducted at Yale in 2012, the researchers found that while respondents were handling a hot pack, they reported having fewer ill thoughts about a previous encounter in which they were lonely. (They also discovered that lonely persons prefer to take longer showers at a higher temperature.) The researchers argue that a temporary remedy can substitute physical temperature for emotional warmth; however, they caution that this should not be allowed to take the place of genuine human connection in the long term.

Recast Your Circumstances In Your Mind

According to Winch, it will be difficult to divert your attention away from ruminating if the need to do so is extraordinarily strong. Therefore, before you even attempt it, it is highly recommended that you mentally rethink or reevaluate the scenario. Don't dwell on the fact that you won't be able to go anywhere or do anything if, for example, your flight is canceled, and you must wait hours. Consider it an opportunity to get some work done or pick up the phone and talk to your folks or perhaps an old friend. After successfully reframing the scenario, it may be simpler to divert yourself by engaging in a visualization exercise (such as Winch's "item list" exercise), reading a book, doing a crossword puzzle, or going for a short walk.

Additional Suggestions To Help Reduce Unproductive Thinking

Start repaying closer attention to what is going through your head. For instance, if you find that you are having negative thoughts because of receiving criticism, you should first become aware of what your mind creates. When you become conscious of your line of thinking, you unlock the ability to modify the influence those thoughts have on your feelings and actions. Compassion should be your response to your thoughts. When you answer to thought with compassion, you can discover that this caring and kinder approach lessens the distressing emotions you're experiencing. Compassion brings about a greater knowledge and acceptance of our existing state and a calming effect on the autonomic nervous system. Keep your attention on the things that are most important to you. We can't guarantee that your defeatism will stop, but you can commit to focusing on the things that matter in your life. Concentrate on the thing that you have power over your actions. For instance, if you think, "I will fail at a new work," you should engage in activities congruent with why you decided to look for a new career. You may enjoy a good challenge, a sense of adventure, expanding your knowledge, and financial flexibility. Despite believing you will fail; you should still engage in behaviors representing these ideals. Even though you are having negative thoughts, you are always in control of your behaviors. Negative thought processes are natural components of the thinking process in humans. How we react to these thoughts is what matters. Only at that point will the negative thoughts have less of an effect on how you function.

Chapter 6: Overcoming Self-destructive Habits

"The atomic bomb was created with the destruction of men in mind"— Bangambiki Habyarimana

You undoubtedly have a history of engaging in behaviors that are damaging to you. Most people do. Most of the time, it is not deliberate and does not develop into a habit. In this context, "self-destructive behaviors" refer to actions that are certain to hurt a person's mental or physical health. Another possibility is that you are fully aware of what you are doing but cannot resist the temptation because it is too intense. It is also possible that it is associated with a mental health problem, such as anxiety or depression.

What does it mean to engage in self-destructive behavior?

When an individual engages in actions that are certain to result in emotional or bodily injury to themselves, this is an example of self-destructive conduct. Some forms of self-destructive conduct are more evident than others, such as binge eating or attempting suicide.

- consuming obsessive behaviors such as betting, gaming, or shopping

- engaging in sexual conduct that is impulsive and potentially dangerous

- overusing drugs and alcohol

- self-injury, including but not limited to cutting, pulling out hair, and burning

There are other more covert methods of sabotaging one's efforts. It's possible that, on cognitive awareness, you're not even aware that you're doing it. The following are some examples of maladaptive behaviors:

- being self-derogatory

- insisting that you are not smart, capable, or attractive enough

- adjusting yourself to please others

- clinging to a person who is not interested in you

- engaging in aggressive or alienating behavior that pushes people away

- engaging in maladaptive activities, such as compulsive evasion, procrastination, and passive-aggressiveness

- and wallowing in self-pity

It varies from individual to individual, depending on how often these behaviors occur. Some people experience them seldom and just mildly, while others may be hazardous.

6.1: Insecurities

Insecurities impact our lives in every way. Insecurities about our appearance, height, vocal quality, and other factors are common.

Bullying at school or obsessively perusing social media and evaluating yourself against others can contribute to insecurities. Daily occurrences can make us feel inadequate, or past experiences can haunt us in the present and undermine our confidence.

A low sense of self-worth may be the root of our insecurities.

They result from negative self-talk, which centers on self-doubt and self-image concerns. When we don't value and practice self-care, we frequently feel insecure.

Various insecurities

We should be aware of a few anxieties as they may affect various facets of our life. Consider the following three sorts of insecurities:

1. Personal unease

Personal insecurities include your appearance, voice, and how others see you. To someone outdoors looking in, these superficial anxieties – fretting about hair, dress, or an unpleasant blemish — may appear trivial.

However, they may be distressing and lead a person to feel intensely. If we allow them, our doubts may even stop us from seeking friendships, romantic relationships, or professional chances.

They may be caused by a lack of confidence due to your intense concern for what other folks think of you. They often but not always have to do with body image.

People often use social media sites to compare themselves to others and feed their fears, which may lead to harmful coping techniques, including eating disorders or self-harm.

2. Uncertainty in the workplace

At work, people have professional fears that make them uncomfortable and self-conscious while speaking out or giving presentations.

People who suffer from these fears may also feel self-conscious and unqualified for risk-taking or advancement. It causes impostor syndrome and prevents individuals from reaching their objectives.

3. Uncertainty in relationships

Any relationship might have frequent relationship anxieties. They give you the impression someone else will be happy and that you don't deserve your relationship.

These anxieties may result in envy, disputes, or aggressive conduct. Relationship concerns may result from prior traumatic experiences with ex-partners, other friends, or family members.

6.2: Ways to Improve Insecurities

It is impossible to discover a single solution that would work for everyone's fears; people are insecure for various reasons. If some of your techniques aren't producing the desired results, you may need to consider other options. Keeping this in mind, the following is a list of ten suggestions that can assist you in overcoming your insecurities:

- Confronting your emotions rather than avoiding them is the better option.

- Maintain a development mentality and organize your objectives carefully.

- Be ready for failures, but don't give in to the temptation to let them dictate your actions.

- Accept and celebrate all your unique qualities and interests.

- Think critically and combat the bad ideas you've been

having.

- Put yourself in situations where upbeat, supportive individuals surround you.

- Take the time to hear other people's experiences conquering their fears and doubts.

- Experiment with new activities that bring you joy.

- Let's eliminate the people and circumstances that contribute to your insecurity.

No matter how great or tiny your achievements may be, you should be pleased with your development.

Consequences of Insecurities

We all have bad days but dwelling on the negative for an extended period may significantly influence your life. It is detrimental to both our physical and emotional well-being. Because our anxieties are rooted in how we feel about ourselves, having a lot of insecurities that dominate our thoughts might lead to a lack of confidence in ourselves.

Low self-esteem may put us at higher risk for various mental health problems, including increased anxiety and depression. We cannot have faith in ourselves when our sense of self-worth is poor and weak. It might cause us to give up on our goals and settle for a more comfortable life.

It is powerful to have a good self-image, yet we tend to be too critical of ourselves when it is taken away. It has the potential to make individuals completely disregard their capacity for self-compassion.

Even narcissists suffer from feelings of inadequacy. Narcissistic individuals often engage in a behavior known as "flexing" to make up for feelings of inadequacy.

Insecurities may also be problematic for the relationships in our lives. The insecurity may lead to other negative emotions, such as mistrust, anger, and even hatred toward our friends, families, and lovers. If this behavior is not addressed and rectified, it will inevitably lead to tension, which is not good for anybody involved.

Your insecurities cannot dictate the terms of your existence in any way. Contact one of the expert coaches here at BetterUp if you need assistance conquering your fears to take control of your life. We would be more than happy to assist you in gaining perspective and teaching you how to learn to lead a life that goes beyond your anxieties.

6.3: Overcoming Self-sabotaging

The term "self-sabotage" refers to the thoughts and actions that we engage in that keep us from realizing our ambitions, desires, and dreams. It is a perfectly natural element of human life, as well as something that every one of us does from time to time—and most of the time, we don't even fully realize that we're doing it. The good news is that it is conceivable to conquer a harsh inner critic if you are familiar with the many forms of self-sabotage, the sources from which it originates, and some useful strategies to counteract it.

People that participate in self-sabotage tend to engage in self-defeating activities consistently. These behaviors may include procrastination, rigidity, negative self-talk, avoiding confrontation, or conflict avoidance. They undercut their attempts to develop the life they desire, often fueled by worry, fear, and self-doubt. When comportment becomes a habit, it is performed so effortlessly that you don't even fully recognize you're doing it or that it's directly leading to bad results. It is when the issue of self-sabotage becomes very severe.

Warning Signs That You're Sabotaging Yourself

People often aren't even informed that they are sabotaging themselves, but when you look more closely, it might appear like avoidance, the production of conflict, or dominating conduct. You may start modifying those ways as soon as you realize how you sabotage yourself.

Included in the list of eleven indications of self-sabotage is a pattern of the following behaviors:

- Keeping your distance from individuals and circumstances that give you an uneasy feeling

- Maintaining the status quo and resisting change are both bad ideas.

- lowering one's sights in pursuit of achievement by setting objectives that are too modest

- causing strife with one's significant other, loved ones, acquaintances, or colleagues

- attempting to exercise one's dominance over other people

- Trying to win the approval of other people

- Making excuses

- Taking behaviors that are at odds with your principles and the objectives you've set for yourself

- Putting oneself in other people's shoes

- Withdrawal from society or solitary existence

- Risky habits

6.4: How to Avoid Sabotaging Your Success

It is feasible to replace self-sabotage with self-advancement since it is not an intrinsic part of your character and does not define who you are or wipe out your qualities and abilities. Begin with the most basic self-improvement tactics and progressively layer on more complex strategies until your inner voice no longer stands in the way of your success and pleasure.

Here are eight things you may do to quit undermining your efforts:

1. Raise Your Level of Self-Awareness

Devote some of your time to introspection so that you may become more self-aware of how you sabotage yourself. You could find it helpful to keep a notebook regularly to track your habits and mental patterns and determine the source of these tendencies. Take some time off for some self-reflection at many points during the day. You will be able to become more deliberate about the areas of your life that require you to adjust as you get more understanding of yourself.

2. Take a Step Back Before You Jump

This ancient saying offers applicable advice for those who undermine themselves in today's world. When you become aware of unfavorable behavior patterns, thoughts, and emotions, it is important to examine whether these routines serve you or work against you. It is common for us to feel forced to perform a task (or to avoid and do something) out of fear; thus, taking a minute to assess whether a situation will hold you back or advance you ahead might prevent you from sabotaging your efforts.

3. Establish Goals That Have Meaning For You and Combine Them With just an Action Plan

Having meaningful objectives might assist you in living with more purpose. Combining relevant objectives with attainable steps might be even more effective. When determining your objectives, keep in mind the things that are most important to you. What attributes/characteristics of your life that you wish were different? What factors promote/contribute to developing a feeling of purpose and meaning? What gives you a sense of vitality & brings out the best in you? The next stage is to determine what manageable actions you could take to make progress toward a goal.

4. Introduce Some Minor Alterations

Taking constructive action is preferable to counterproductive actions toward one's goals but remember that changing habits requires taking baby steps. Consider the idea of making changes on a more gradual scale. Replace a thought or activity with another daily and allow yourself enough time for the replacement to become a habit.

5. Befriend Yourself

Because the inner critic is one of the key factors contributing to self-sabotage, one of the most important steps in the process of halting self-sabotage is replacing habitual, self-critical thoughts with more loving ones. By admitting your feelings and embracing your errors from the past as a natural part of the human experience, you may cultivate a compassionate and accepting attitude toward yourself.

6. Recognize and Make Use of Your Strengths

Once recognized, acknowledged, and accepted, each person's character qualities have the potential to help them flourish in life. Think about the things you're good at, the skills you possess, the values you uphold, and the feelings of success you enjoy. When do you feel your best? Self-love may be developed by awareness of one's strengths and pursuing activities that put those qualities, or at least one, to use daily.

7. Make a habit out of being mindful.

The practice of mindfulness refers to a way of living that emphasizes being completely present and rooted in the here and now. It assists you in differentiating the events of the past from those of the present and ideas from actuality. It allows you to select how to react to a person or circumstance that challenges you.

8. Consult a Counselor Specialized in Mental Health

A therapist may help you better understand yourself by guiding you kindlier. They also share advice and tactics for starting down self-sabotaging ideas and finding ways to strengthen your psychological self-care. Find a psychotherapist that you get along with well and start making changes in your life as soon as you can later doing so.

6.5: Activities to reduce anxiety

You are not the only one coping with anxiety if you or somebody you know is experiencing it. According to some studies, nearly forty percent of adults and ten percent of adolescents in the United States suffer from an anxiety condition of some kind. Anxiety is a problem that affects people of every age and may start as young as 18 months for neonates. However, anxiety symptoms often become more obvious when a person is a teenager. Anxiety, when it reaches a certain level of severity, can be debilitating and may significantly impact mood and life.

It is essential to speak with a mental health expert when the possibility of having an anxiety problem is present. Professionals in the mental health field are highly knowledgeable in mental illness, social behavior, and psychiatric rehabilitation. They can conduct an exhaustive assessment and guide the most effective treatment options and methods for managing anxiety. Emerge is a psychiatric clinic in the Denver metropolitan region that focuses on behavioral health and offers several treatment choices for those struggling with anxiety disorder.

In addition to seeking therapy for one's mental health, an individual may also wish to engage in activities that help relieve anxiety. Several hobbies and exercises may help lower stress, make you feel better and more optimistic, and make it leisurely for you to manage anxiety. These benefits can all come from reducing stress. Here is a summary of some straightforward actions that you may use to control anxiety in the comfort of one's home.

1. Take a ride or stroll your bike around at a leisurely pace. Endorphins are a kind of chemical released into the body due to physical exercise. Endorphins have been shown to enhance sleep function, induce sensations of happiness, and decrease stress.

2. Keep a notebook of your thoughts. Keeping a journal is an exceptional method for articulating your thoughts and releasing them into paper in a tangible form. Putting your ideas on paper may help you gain clarity and transform unpleasant sentiments into strong beliefs that can affect your mood.

3. Meditate or practice yoga. Medical professionals increasingly recommend yoga and meditation to treat anxiety and stress. Being mindful of your breath or concentrating on a meditative thought might assist you in being present and lessen the intensity of anxious sensations.

4. Take in some musical sounds. If you listen to music, you might divert your attention away from troubling ideas and find yourself in a more upbeat frame of mind. The tendency

of slow, classical music to generate a relaxing effect is one of the genre's most well-known strengths.

5. Try learning/reading a book or going to the movies. It is helpful to keep your mind off stressful events and chores by doing something enjoyable like reading a light novel or watching a movie. You should do this while watching a movie or reading a book with an uplifting message or central subject.

Conclusion

Most people, at some moment/point in their lives, have pondered the question of how to move on from a painful previous experience. It is only natural/normal for you to feel that the source of the emotional agony you are experiencing now lies in the past. However, even if it happened in the past, the first step in overcoming the pain is concentrating on the present. Everyone will likely interpret the question of how to move on from the past differently. It could also depend on the circumstances of the case. You could believe that letting go means revisiting painful situations or individuals without feeling the associated emotional pain. It's possible that you feel like it's about forgetting everything. Alternatively, it could suggest that you wish to move on even though you haven't forgotten or forgiven the person yet. It is possible to let go of whatever is weighing heavily on your heart and head, whatever that may mean to you. You can rehabilitate, and the following advice may be of assistance to you. If you dwell on the pain, you risk doing much more damage to yourself overall. It is essential to acquire the skills necessary to cope with that sorrow, to put that specific circumstance in history, and to heal oneself by clinging solely to those things that will enable one to develop and progress in life. Even though it may appear simple, letting go of something is sometimes one of the most difficult things a person can do. We both know this. Leaving the past in the past & concentrating on the present situation will make room for new experiences to enter your life. It will clear your mind of all the negative feelings and allow you to make room for new thoughts that will contribute to your growth. As you accept joy and love into your heart with open arms, you will soon understand that getting going was the wisest option you could have made because you will soon know that letting go was the finest option you could have made.

One Final Step

Honest reviews of my books help bring them to the attention of other readers.

If you enjoy this book I would be very grateful if you could spend a few minutes

leaving a review (no matter the length)

Thanks in advance for your support.

A Gift For You

As promised, It is my pleasure to give you a small notebook,

as a thank you for your trust.

I hope it will be helpful to you...

Click Here

or frame the Qr-code to download it.

Make good use of it!

References

- https://medium.com/the-mission/11-simple-ways-to-stop-overthinking-everything-and-take-control-of-your-life-cf6de0b8d83f

- https://www.medicalnewstoday.com/articles/162035#what-is-anger-management

- https://www.verywellmind.com/how-to-change-negative-thinking-3024843

- https://myonlinetherapy.com/how-to-stop-negative-thoughts-anxiety/

- https://sageclinic.org/blog/negative-thoughts-depression/

- https://melliobrien.com/the-four-keys-to-overcoming-negative-thinkingfor-good/

- https://www.mcleanhospital.org/essential/negative-thinking

- https://www.healthline.com/health/mental-health/intrusive-thoughts#types

- https://www.happify.com/hd/stop-dwelling-on-negative-thoughts/

- https://www.winchesterhospital.org/health-library/article?id=14266

- https://www.goalcast.com/self-esteem-self-love-how-to-love-yourself/#:~:text=Self%2Desteem%20is%20a%20perception,how%20you%20relate%20to%20yourself.

- https://thedailyguru.com/powerful-activities-will-boost-self-esteem/

- https://www.betterup.com/blog/self-love

- https://www.betterup.com/blog/how-to-overcome-insecurities

https://www.choosingtherapy.com/self-sabotaging/

Printed by BoD™in Norderstedt, Germany